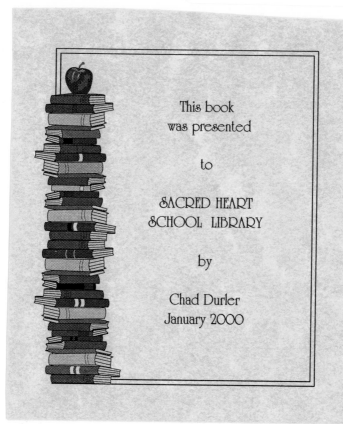

This book
was presented

to

SACRED HEART
SCHOOL LIBRARY

by

Chad Durler
January 2000

A Children's Book About

# BEING CARELESS

Grolier Enterprises, Inc. offers a varied selection of children's
book racks and tote bags. For details on ordering, please write:
Grolier Enterprises Inc., Sherman Turnpike, Danbury, CT 06816
Attn: Premium Department

**Managing Editor: Ellen Klarberg**
**Copy Editor: Annette Gooch**
**Editorial Assistant: Lana Eberhard**
**Art Director: Jennifer Wiezel**
**Production Artist: Gail Miller**
**Illustration Designer: Bartholomew**
**Inking Artist: Susie Hornig**
**Coloring Artist: Susie Hornig**
**Lettering Artist: Linda Hanney**
**Typographer: Communication Graphics**

Printed in 1990

A Children's Book About

# BEING CARELESS

## By Joy Berry

GROLIER ENTERPRISES CORP.

This book is about Lennie.

Reading about Lennie can help you understand and deal with **being careless.**

You are being careless when you act as if you do not care about yourself.

You are being careless when you act as if you do not care about the people and things around you.

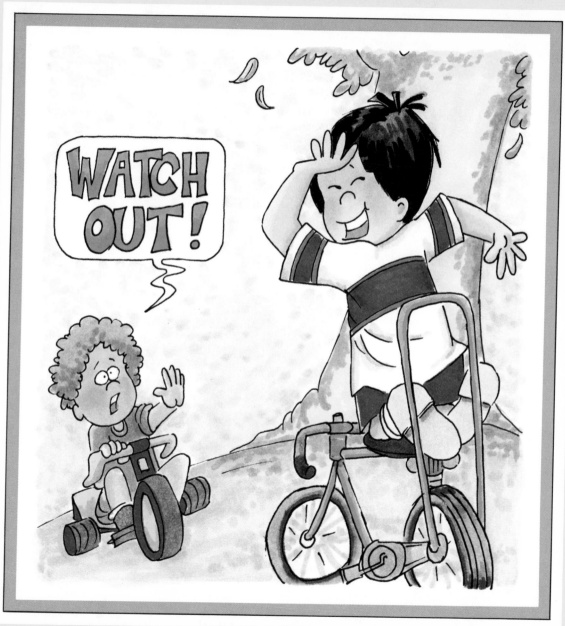

Being careless can cause you to hurt
yourself.

Being careless can cause you to hurt other people.

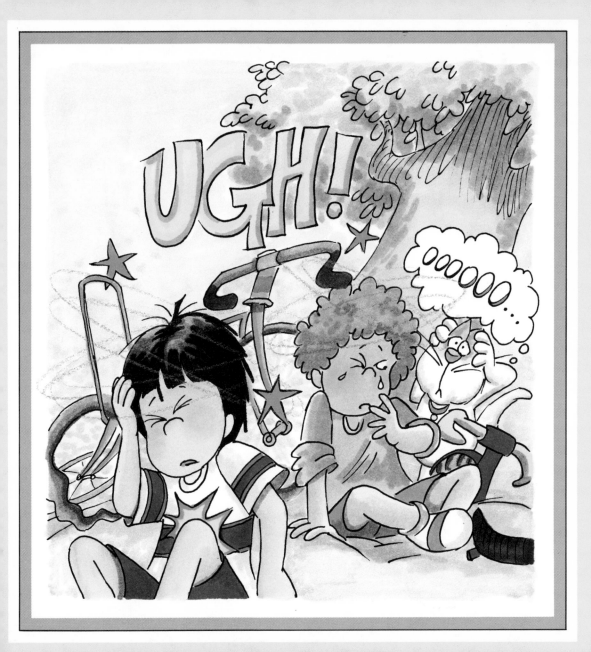

Being careless can cause you to damage or destroy things.

It is not good to be careless.

You need to *be careful* instead.

When you are careful, you act as if you care about yourself.

When you are careful, you act as if you care about the people and things around you.

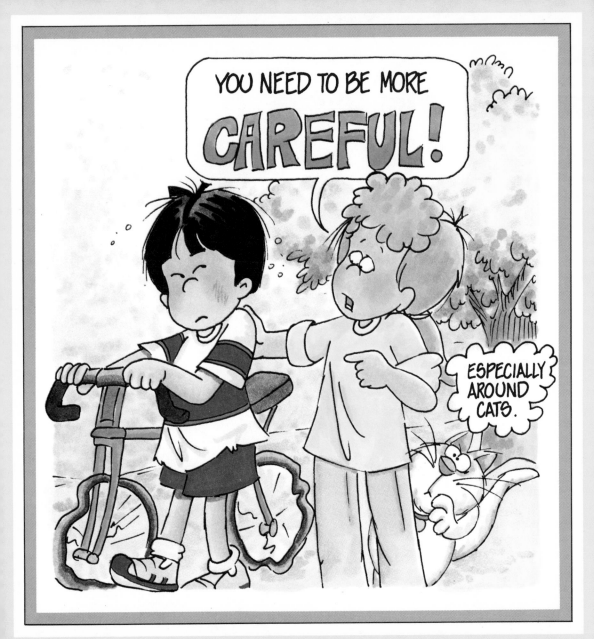

Be careful.

*Obey the rules.*

Your parents usually know what you need to do to keep yourself and others safe. They usually know what you need to do to take care of the things around you.

The rules they make can help you be careful.

Be careful.

*Pay attention to what you do* so you will make fewer mistakes.

Be careful.

*Slow down* so you can avoid accidents and mistakes that happen when you hurry.

Be careful.

*Watch where you are going* so you can avoid tripping and bumping into things.

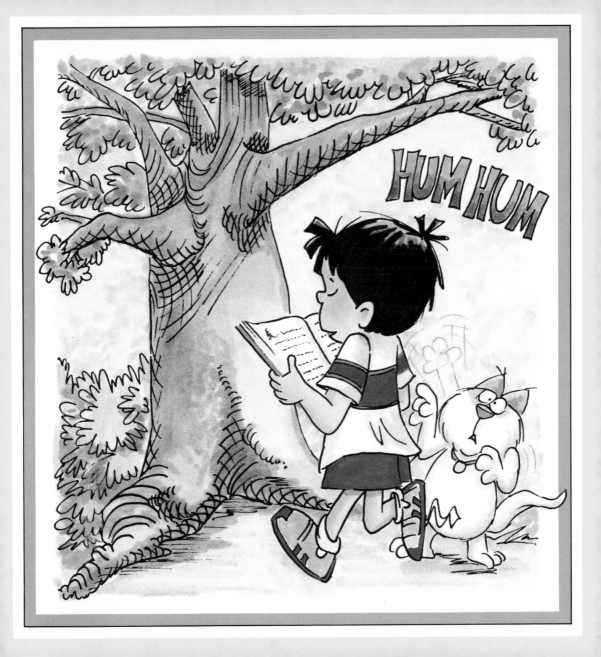

Be careful.

*Be aware of people and things around you* so you can avoid dangerous situations.

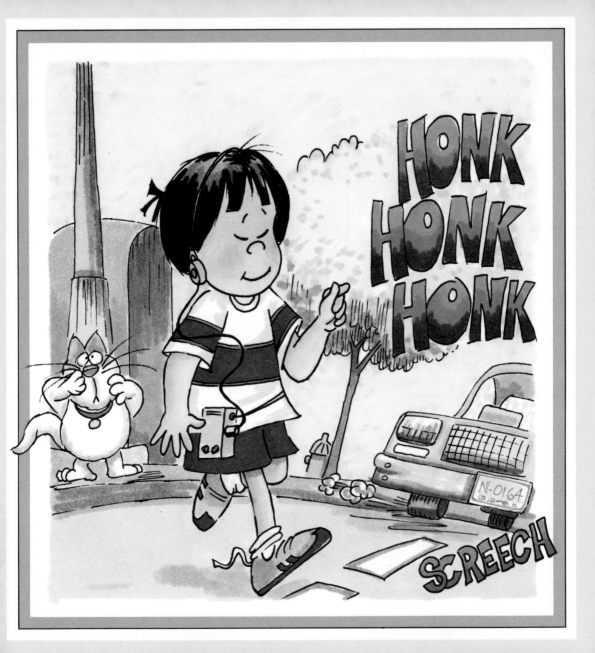

Be careful.

*Avoid playing roughly* so no one will get hurt and nothing will get broken.

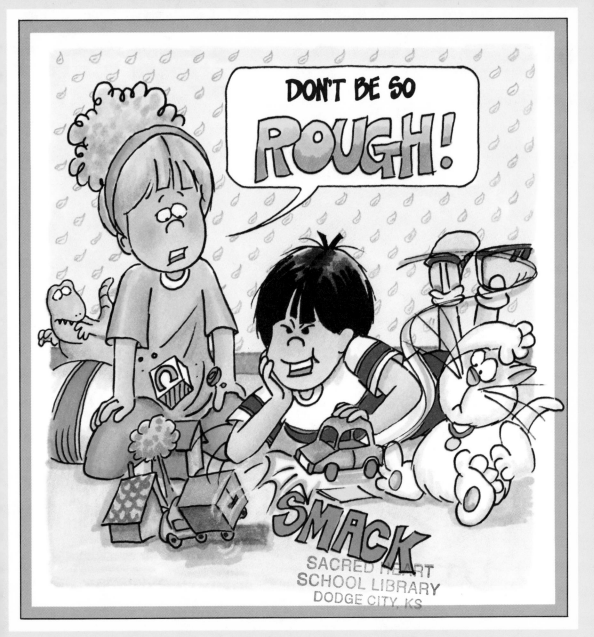

Be careful.

*Avoid playing with dangerous things* so you will not hurt yourself or others.

Be careful.

*Avoid playing in dangerous places* so you will not hurt yourself or others.

Being careless is not good for you or the people around you.

It is better when you are careful.

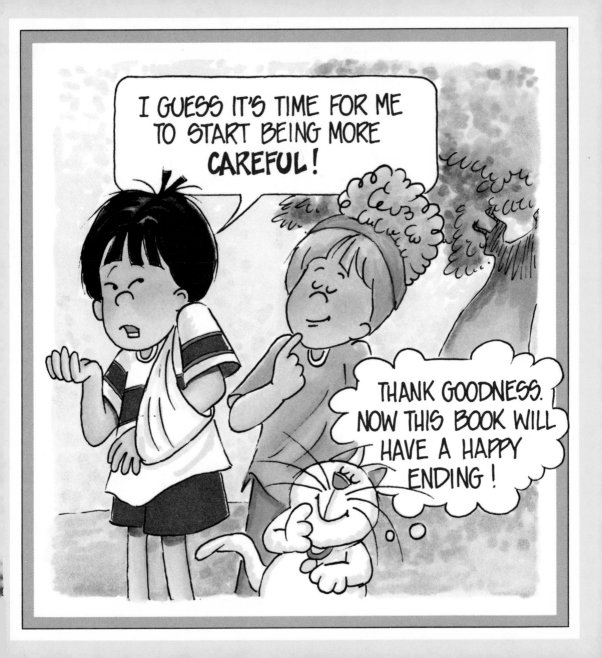